HOW TO
AVOID
WITCHES

PUFFIN BOOKS

UK|USA|Canada|Ireland|Australia
India|New Zealand|South Africa

Puffin Books is part of the Penguin Random House group of companies
whose addresses can be found at global.penguinrandomhouse.com.

www.penguin.co.uk   www.puffin.co.uk   www.ladybird.co.uk

Penguin
Random House
UK

First published 2020
001

Written by Kay Woodward
The Witches: first published 1983
Boy: first published 1984
Copyright © The Roald Dahl Story Company Ltd / Quentin Blake, 1983, 1984, 2020

ROALD DAHL is a registered trademark of The Roald Dahl Story Company Ltd
www.roalddahl.com

Typeset in Aleo, Futura and Russisch Brot by Perfect Bound Ltd
Printed and bound in Great Britain by Clays Ltd, Elcograf S.p.A.
A CIP catalogue record for this book is available from the British Library

ISBN: 978-0-241-46179-2

All correspondence to:
Puffin Books
Penguin Random House Children's
One Embassy Gardens, 8 Viaduct Gardens
London SW11 7BW

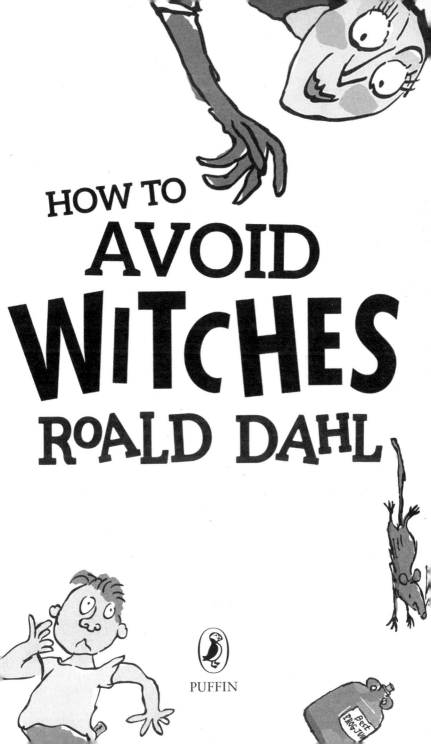

HOW TO
AVOID
WITCHES
ROALD DAHL

PUFFIN

Contents

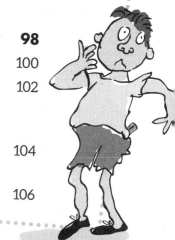

ALL ABOUT
WITCHES

Y ou probably think you know **ALL** about witches. Witches wear pointy black hats and billowing black cloaks. They soar through the night sky on broomsticks. Their cats are *always* black. And every single witch in the world likes nothing more than making her enemies disappear in a puff of smoke.

Right?

WRONG. (Well, most of it. The bit about the puff of smoke is 100 per cent true. Eek!)

The truth is that witches do NOT dress in black outfits and shriek 'woo-ha-ha' a lot, just so you can stare, point and shout, 'CRIKEY! IT'S A WITCH!' at the top of your voice. Instead, witches hide. And they came up with a brilliant plan that guaranteed they would be the trickiest beings to spot on the entire planet.*

---

*Apart from leopards and nosy teachers, who are also very good at staying under the radar until they POUNCE.

REAL WITCHES dress in ordinary clothes and look very much like ordinary women. They live in ordinary houses and they work in ORDINARY JOBS.

Yikes.

But that's not all. There is one more very important thing you need to know about witches before you turn the page.

Witches **HATE** children.

Double yikes.

You **REALLY DON'T** want a witch to find you. And that's why we've written this book: the ultimate guide to avoiding witches. It's filled with all sorts of useful advice and packed with activities, important information from the original story, games and bonus material.

Once you've reached the last page, you'll be qualified to avoid **ALL** witches.

Well, fingers crossed – your life *might* depend on it.

REAL
WITCHES

For all you know, a witch might be living
next door to you right now. Or she might
be the woman with the bright eyes who sat
opposite you on the bus this morning.
She might be the lady with the dazzling smile
who offered you a sweet from a white
paper bag in the street before lunch.

WHICH IS A WITCH?

Which lady is the witch? That is a difficult question, but it is one that every child must try to answer.

'Hmm,' you might be thinking to yourself right now. 'Surely it can't be **THAT** difficult to identify a witch. I'm 100 per cent sure that I could pick a witch out of a line-up.'

Well, guess what? Now's your chance to prove it! Simply study the suspected witches on the opposite page. Read all about them. Use a magnifying glass to look really closely, if you like. Then choose: which lady **IS** a witch? Easy, eh?

Brenda is a librarian who reads three novels a week (five, if she's on holiday). Her favourite meal is spaghetti bolognese and cheesecake. She's allergic to hamsters.

Eunice is a civil engineer. At weekends, she rescues kittens from trees. She likes nothing better than relaxing in a huge squishy armchair with a hot chocolate and a sudoku puzzle.

Linda is a member of an art group and a book group. She puts on sparkly shoes and goes ballroom dancing twice a week. Her sticky toffee pudding won first prize at the village fete.

ANSWER

REVEALED: Brenda, Eunice and Linda are all witches. Yes, really. ALL OF THEM.

7

HOW TO SPOT A WITCH

Witches might look ordinary, but you can find them in a crowd . . . if you know how. Keep an eye out for these warning signs and you just might be able to spot a witch **BEFORE SHE SPOTS YOU**. (This is important, as it will mean you have time to escape.)

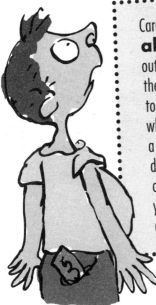

Carry this handy checklist with you **at all times** and practise looking out for witches. Remember, some of these characteristics are very common to women who aren't witches, too, which is why it's so hard to spot a real witch. The thing is, women don't usually have **ALL SIX** characteristics. If you've ticked all six, you can be pretty positive that it's a witch you see before you.

Witches' **EYES** are very different from ours. The pupils are not black. They keep changing colour! (Gosh.)

Witches are totally bald, so they wear **WIGS** to disguise this fact. They only wear first-class wigs, however, which look a lot like real hair.

Witches have **SLIGHTLY LARGER NOSE-HOLES** than you or me. The rim of each nose-hole is pink and curvy.

Witches have **NO TOES AT ALL**. They must hide their wide, square feet in pretty shoes that are far too tight. As a result, they may LIMP VERY SLIGHTLY.

Witches always wear **GLOVES**, even in summer. This is because, instead of fingernails, they have thin curvy claws and they want to hide them. (Claws would be a bit of a giveaway, don't you agree?)

Witches also have **BLUE-TINGED TEETH**. (Turn the page to find out why.)

FRIGHTENINGLY **FEARFUL** FACTS:

BLUE SPIT

There is a **simple reason** witches' teeth are tinged with blue. It's **not** because they have been sucking everlasting gobstoppers. They **haven't** been licking blueberry ice lollies, either. And it **isn't** because they've been chewing bright blue felt-tip pens (even though they've been told a million times not to). No, every witch has slightly bluish teeth because . . .

witches have blue spit.

They really do.
It's **totally** true.

Did you know . . .?

While your spit might be wonderfully see-through, a witch's spit is bilberry* blue – a sort of purplish navy blue.

Blue spit makes great ink. Witches write with old-fashioned fountain pens, but, instead of filling them up with ink, they simply lick the nib.

Witches **NEVER** spit. Because why on earth would they? They may as well just wear a T-shirt with the words **I AM A REAL WITCH** written in blue-spit ink!

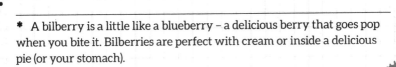

---

* A bilberry is a little like a blueberry – a delicious berry that goes pop when you bite it. Bilberries are perfect with cream or inside a delicious pie (or your stomach).

THE WITCHES' MOTTO

Are you ready? Prepare yourself.

This is the motto that all witches live by:

One child a week is fifty-two a year.

Squish them and squiggle them and make them disappear.

Unfortunately, it's **true**.

A witch's number-one enemy is:

YOU.

This is why it's especially important that you keep out of a witch's way. You don't want to be squished or squiggled by a witch, do you? And we're guessing that there's a fairly good chance you don't want to disappear either.

WRITE YOUR OWN
(anti-witch) MOTTO!

**Can you do better than the witches?
Now's your chance to try!**

Use the grim and gruesome selection of
words opposite to fill in the gaps and create
your own brand-new **anti-witch** motto.
Choose a word from each numbered set to
fill in the corresponding blank.

1 _____ **them and**

2 _____ **them and
make them**

3 _____

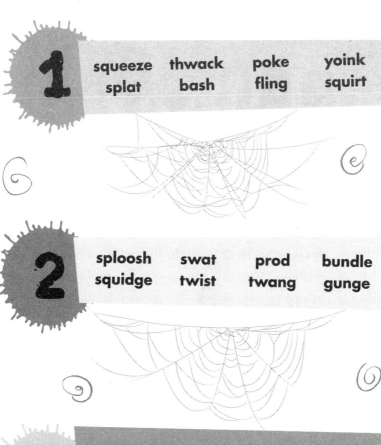

1

squeeze thwack poke yoink
splat bash fling squirt

2

sploosh swat prod bundle
squidge twist twang gunge

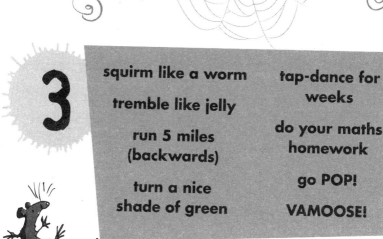

3

squirm like a worm

tremble like jelly

run 5 miles
(backwards)

turn a nice
shade of green

tap-dance for
weeks

do your maths
homework

go POP!

VAMOOSE!

15

WICKEDLY
BAD JOKES

Prepare yourself. These jokes are 100 per cent awful, just like witches.

What does a witch use to create a really wild hairdo?
Scarespray.

How do you make a witch itch?
Cross out the 'w'.

What do you call a witch at the seaside?
A sand-witch.

What noise does a witch make when she flies very, very fast?
Brrrroom-brrrroom.

How many witches does it take to change a lightbulb?
It depends – what are they changing the lightbulb into?

Did you hear about the witches who shared a flat?
They were broom-mates.

17

THE GRAND HIGH WITCH

'She is the ruler of them all,'
my grandmother said.
'She is all-powerful. She is without
mercy. All other witches are
petrified of her.'

FACT FILE:
THE GRAND HIGH WITCH

Occupation: Witch, obviously.

Height: Tiny – probably no more than four and a half feet tall.

Age: About twenty-five or twenty-six.

Wears: A rather stylish long black dress, which is so long (or she's so short) that it reaches right to the ground.

Also wears: Black gloves that come up to her elbows.

What do you think of The Grand High Witch? She doesn't look **SO** bad, does she? Rate her scariness on this handy **SCARE-O-METER**.

a little bit
scary

quite
chilling

Of course, this isn't really what The Grand High Witch looks like. She's **MUCH MORE TERRIFYING**. Turn the page to discover her true appearance, which she hides underneath her disguise . . .

BUT ONLY IF YOU ARE BRAVE ENOUGH.

knee-tremblingly
nerve-racking .... pretty
petrifying .... FEARFULLY
FRIGHTENING

THE GRAND HIGH WITCH . . .

UNMASKED!

There are times when something is so frightful you become mesmerized by it and can't look away.

Ta-daaaaaaaaa . . . **arrrrrghhhhh!**

GULP.

Isn't she GHASTLY?

Isn't she GRIM?

Isn't she the most GRUESOME creature you've ever seen?

(Just in case you are wondering, the answer to all three questions is **YES**.)

We have helpfully labelled some of the very scariest bits of The Grand High Witch. But there's room for you to add your own captions! Make sure they're properly horrible, though. There is NOTHING nice about The Grand High Witch.

A look of serpents in her eyes.

The skin around her mouth and cheeks is cankered and worm-eaten, as though maggots are working away in there.

A face so crumpled and wizened, so shrunken and shrivelled, it looks as though it has been pickled in vinegar.*

Her mask hooks on behind her ears. It is SO easy to remove!

---

* Oops. We forgot to check. Are you eating anything that's been pickled in vinegar right now? Maybe a crunchy gherkin or a pickled onion that's making your eyes water? If so, you might want to screw the lid back on the jar. Save your delicious vinegary nibbles for another day, when you're NOT reading about The Grand High Witch. Otherwise, she might put you off for life.

The Grand High Witch's
DICTIONARY
OF INSULTS

The Grand High Witch doesn't waste her time complimenting other people. She is far too wicked for that. Instead, she prefers to devote her energy to peppering her audience with a range of – frankly, soul-crushing – insults.

Blithering bumpkin

A bumpkin is a rather socially awkward person from the countryside who is not used to the shiny, loud excitement of a city. Blithering means utter, complete or total.

Boshvolloping suggestion

A totally nonsensical suggestion. (We think.)

Brrrainless bogvumper

You can probably work out brrrainless on your own. And who knows what a bogvumper is?! (We're certainly not going to ask The Grand High Witch to tell us.)

Tomfiddling idea

A ridiculous idea. (Probably.)

PRRRONUNCIATION

The eagle-eyed among you will have noticed strrraight away that one of the insults on page 25 wasn't spelled quite rrright. WELL SPOTTED. *Brrrainless* is spelled this way because that's how The Grand High Witch says it. She loves to rrroll her Rs.

If you've never learned how to rrroll your Rs (and if you're not The Grand High Witch then it's quite prrrobable that you haven't), it's very simple and requires no magic at all.

Here's how:

1. Open your mouth.
2. Lift your tongue until it is nearly touching the roof of your mouth.
3. Now say: 'Errrrrr.'
4. Hurrrah! You are now rrrolling your Rs. It is incredibly similar to the sound a car makes when it goes over a cattle grrrid.

BRRRAVO!

Now practise your brrrand-new rrrolling skill by saying The Grand High Witch's words many, many times to anyone who will listen.

FRIGHTENINGLY **FEARFUL** FACTS:

FRIZZLING

Sometimes other people do just annoy you. When this happens, you might:

a) Tut loudly.

b) Roll your eyes and say, 'You twit.'

c) Shout, 'STOP THAT AT ONCE, YOU BLITHERING NINCOMPOOP!'

But if you're The Grand High Witch, you probably won't do any of the above. Instead, you'll:

d) FRIZZLE THEM LIKE A FRITTER.

How to frizzle someone like a fritter (or cook them like a carrot)

It's really quite easy (as long as you're The Grand High Witch – if you're not The Grand High Witch, it will be a little more difficult). Simply point a gloved finger at the unfortunate soul who's annoyed you, then **STARE** at them.

Frizzzzzzzzzzzzle!

That's the sound made by a stream of sparks shooting out of The Grand High Witch's eyes and hurtling through the air towards her target. The sparks look just like tiny white-hot metal-filings. They are really quite pretty, if you like that sort of thing.

And, just like that, your victim will disappear.

WARNING: Frizzling is likely to produce a puff of smoke and the distinct smell of burning meat. Do not worry. This is completely normal and absolutely nothing to be concerned about. (Unless you're the one being frizzled, of course.)

THE GRAND HIGH ~~WITCH~~ QUIZ

Are YOU as scary as The Grand High Witch? Take this fun quiz to find out!

1 Are you tall enough to ...

a) reach the cake tins in the very highest kitchen cupboard without standing on a younger sibling?

b) look a maths teacher in the eye?

c) only just see over the edge of the bathroom sink?

2 If you stare crossly at someone, do they ...

a) stare crossly back?

b) run away so quickly that they break the sound barrier?

c) disappear in a puff of smoke?

3 What is your favourite type of soup?

a) Tomato soup

b) Mock turtle soup

c) Green-pea soup

4 How far can you kick a football?

a) 3.2 metres

b) 10.4 metres

c) Over the fence, straight through the roof of next-door's greenhouse, down the road and past the shopping centre, where it rebounds off the school wall . . . and comes back again!

5 If you could turn your deadliest enemy into anything you liked, what would you choose?

a) A wombat

b) A tax inspector

c) A mouse

Turn the page to find out how scary you are . . .

THE GRAND HIGH

RESULTS ~~WITCH~~

C ount up how many times you answered a), b) and c) to find out how scary you are compared to The Grand High Witch.

a)

b)

c)

If you answered mostly a)

You are not even a tiny bit scary. Seriously, there are gerbils that are scarier than you. If you were considering making Grand High Witchery a career, think again. You're far better suited to running a toy shop.

If you answered mostly b)

You are reasonably scary. If you dress up as The Grand High Witch for Halloween, you might be spooky enough to make a nervous child go, 'Eeeeek!' You might even make a grown-up squeal. Try it.

If you answered mostly c)

You are so incredibly scary that you might even **BE** The Grand High Witch. Are you sure you're not? Have you checked to see if you have toes recently? Are there hooks behind your ears on which to hang your lovely face? (It's probably best not to check – what if there are?!)

Formula 86 Delayed Action

MOUSE-MAKER

'I vont everybody's attention for I am about to be telling you vot you must do to prepare Formula 86 Delayed Action Mouse-Maker!'

WITCHES'
WEEKLY
Are you a witch?*

Are you fed up with irritating,

pesky, LOUD children?

**Do you want to rid the world of the stinky
smell of dogs' droppings FOREVER?**

Then we have the solution!

FORMULA 86
DELAYED ACTION
MOUSE-MAKER

*Well, of course you are. You wouldn't be reading this otherwise.

This powerful potion is guaranteed to turn troublesome tots and terrible children into — yes, you guessed it — MICE. Keen to be involved? Now's your chance! All you need to do is design a label for our brand-new potion. The designer of the best label will win an all-expenses-paid trip to the home of witchcraft . . . **Norway!**

Terms and conditions: Competition open to all witches over the age of 175. Winner's travel is by economy broomstick only.

FROM **POTION** TO MOUSETRAP

This is Bruno Jenkins. Bruno gobbled up a squishy bar of chocolate that contained a single droplet of Formula 86 Delayed Action Mouse-Maker. At precisely 3.30 p.m. the following day, the potion started to work. Follow the arrows to find out what happened next!

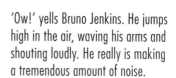

'Ow!' yells Bruno Jenkins. He jumps high in the air, waving his arms and shouting loudly. He really is making a tremendous amount of noise.

That's odd. Is it a trick of the light or is Bruno Jenkins getting smaller? He is absolutely silent and very still, too. If he were playing musical statues, he'd be winning.

Gosh. Bruno Jenkins has grown a tail. And he is most definitely shrinking . . .

Now Bruno Jenkins has whiskers and four tiny feet!

Hmm. Bruno Jenkins isn't looking much like a boy any more, is he? He's terribly furry . . .

In fact, it's looking exceedingly like Bruno Jenkins is a . . . small . . . brown . . .

Squeeeeeeeeeeeeeeak!

MOUSE!

A **DEADLY** SONG

Her Grandness, The Grand High Witch Of All The World, described in her terrifyingly detailed song exactly how Formula 86 Delayed Action Mouse-Maker works . . .

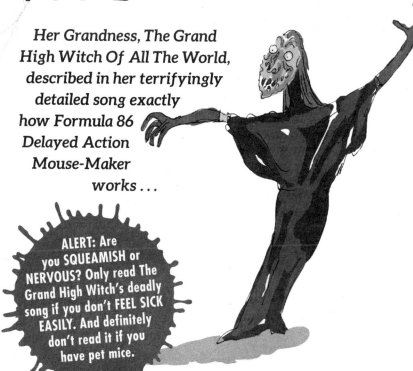

ALERT: Are you SQUEAMISH or NERVOUS? Only read The Grand High Witch's deadly song if you don't FEEL SICK EASILY. And definitely don't read it if you have pet mice.

Down with children! Do them in!
Boil their bones and fry their skin!
Bish them, sqvish them, bash them, mash them!
Brrreak them, shake them, slash them, smash them!
Offer chocs with magic powder!
Say 'Eat up!' then say it louder.
Crrram them full of sticky eats,
Send them home still guzzling sveets.

And in the morning little fools
Go marching off to separate schools.
A girl feels sick and goes all pale.
She yells, 'Hey look! I've grrrown a tail!'
A boy who's standing next to her
Screams, 'Help! I think I'm grrrowing fur!'
Another shouts, 'Vee look like frrreaks!
There's viskers growing on our cheeks!'
A boy who vos extremely tall
Cries out, 'Vot's wrong? I'm grrrowing small!'
Four tiny legs begin to sprrrout
From everybody rrround about.
And all at vunce, all in a trrrice,
There are no children! Only **MICE!**

In every school is mice galore
All rrrunning rrround the school-rrroom floor!
And all the poor demented teachers
Is yelling, 'Hey, who are these crrreatures?'
They stand upon the desks and shout,
'Get out, you filthy mice! Get out!
Vill someone fetch some mousetrrraps, please!
And don't forrrget to bring the cheese!'
Now mousetrrraps come and every trrrap
Goes snippy-snip and snappy-snap.
The mousetrrraps have a powerful spring,
The springs go crack and snap and ping!
Is lovely noise for us to hear!
Is music to a vitch's ear!

Dead mice is every place arrround,
Piled two feet deep upon the grrround,
Vith teachers searching left and rrright,
But not a single child in sight!

The teachers cry, 'Vot's going on?
Oh vhere have all the children gone?
Is half-past nine and as a rrrule
They're never late as this for school!'
Poor teachers don't know vot to do.
Some sit and rrread, and just a few
Amuse themselves throughout the day
By sveeping all the mice avay.
AND ALL US VITCHES SHOUT 'HOORAY!'

HOW TO AVOID

FORMULA 86 DELAYED
ACTION MOUSE-MAKER

*Chances are, you probably don't want to be turned
into a mouse.* It's not for everyone. So, how do
you avoid this happening to you? Don't worry!*

Just follow these simple rules to protect yourself
from one of the dastardliest witch-plots of all time.
(Probably. You'll be at least **85 per cent** safe, anyway.)

1 As witches hide Formula 86 Delayed Action
Mouse-Maker inside delicious chocolate,
the most obvious rule is: **DON'T EAT
CHOCOLATE**. (Sorry. We know chocolate is
extremely difficult to avoid,
but try your best.)

---

*If you think mice are terribly sweet and you rather like the idea of a
lifetime of cheese, then please ignore this VALUABLE ADVICE.

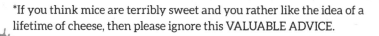

2 If you absolutely have to eat some chocolate, **test it** on grown-ups who you dislike first. (Only give them a little bit. Obviously you'll want to save most of it for yourself.) Once you're sure the chocolate doesn't contain Formula 86 Delayed Action Mouse-Maker, quickly eat the rest.

3 Keep your chocolate **safe**. Guard it with a very fierce dog and a high-security camera system that costs billions. Be especially vigilant at Easter. Just think how much Formula 86 Delayed Action Mouse-Maker a witch could hide inside a chocolate egg ...

Psst! In case you do turn into a mouse, PLAN AHEAD. Talk to your friends (no grown-ups) about the latest humane methods of pest control. You might need to convince your parents to adopt safe mouse-capture methods in your home, but it's worth it. Go on, quick! You REALLY don't want to end up in a snappy mousetrap.

HOME
SQUEAK
HOME

However much you try to avoid Formula 86 Delayed Action Mouse-Maker, there is always a chance that those pesky witches will find a way to trick you into swallowing it.

So why not build your own Marvellous Mouse Mansion in case that happens? Then if you ARE turned into a mouse ... you can move straight in!

Design your new home HERE.

And don't forget to include a Really Big Cheese Fridge. No mouse house is complete without one!

RRRECIPE TIME:
DOUBLE-CHOC FLAPJACKS

Wouldn't it be wonderful if you could eat a chocolatey treat guaranteed to contain no Formula 86 Delayed Action Mouse-Maker whatsoever? You CAN. All you have to do is make it yourself!

You will need:

- 20cm x 20cm baking tin
- Greaseproof paper
- A large saucepan
- A chopping board
- 150g butter
- 150g golden syrup or brown sugar
- 300g jumbo porridge oats
- 50g dark chocolate
- 50g white chocolate

Ask a grown-up to help you with this recipe!

What to do:

1 Preheat the oven to 150°C.

2 Line the baking tin with greaseproof paper.

3 Ask a grown-up to help you melt the butter in a large saucepan over a low heat.

4 Add the golden syrup or brown sugar to the saucepan. Absolutely do not taste the mixture because it will be **HOTTER THAN THE SURFACE OF THE SUN** (or thereabouts).

5 Stir until the sugar has dissolved. Then take the pan off the heat and mix in the porridge oats.

6 Squish the mixture into the lined baking tin.

There's more . . .

7 Pop it in the oven for 40 minutes.

8 Take the tin out of the oven (using oven gloves – **NOT** witches' gloves!) and leave your masterpiece to cool for 20 minutes. Then tip it on to a chopping board. **Make sure you get a grown-up to help with this bit.**

9 Melt the dark chocolate in the microwave. Heat it in a bowl for 20 seconds, then check it. If it's not quite melted, heat it for another 20 seconds. Repeat until it's melted. Do the same for the white chocolate.

10 Drizzle the melted chocolate all over the flapjack slab. Be as artistic as you like. Drizzle a portrait of The Grand High Witch if you must.

11 Ask a grown-up to help you cut the flapjacks into squares.

12 Eat, with **no danger** of turning into a mouse.

The best bit about double-choc flapjacks is that, because they contain oats, grown-ups won't moan about them being unhealthy! (Well, not much anyway.)

FORMULA 86
✳ WORD SEARCH

No, this is NOT a hunt for very slow racing cars. It's a potion-based puzzle!

There are ten ingredients from The Grand High Witch's deadly Formula 86 Delayed Action Mouse-Maker hidden in this dreadfully difficult word search. How many can YOU find?

ALARM CLOCK

BLABBERSNITCH

BROWN MICE

CATSPRINGER

CRABCRUNCHER

FROG JUICE

GROBBLESQUIRT

GRUNTLE'S EGG

MOUSE TAILS

TELESCOPE

```
Y R E G N I R P S T A C Z D
G M W E Z N E O E D C B H B
G O R P J Q U A O U G C R Z
E U E O D N O U M Q T O G P
S S H C O J Q E W I W H P B
E E C S I W F J N N Z S T K
L T N E F B J S M X A L J W
T A U L T G R I L K K J B E
N I R E G E C O A V N X F B
U L C T B E A S R R O W A L
R S B B K C O L C M R A L A
G U A D O L G J P C Z U L P
V L R E Q Z M V D K S T R I
B V C H W H T R H W F L A B
U T R I U Q S E L B B O R G
Y D X E C I U J G O R F G M
```

Answers
on page
144

53

GRAND-MAMMA

My grandmother was Norwegian. The Norwegians know all about witches, for Norway, with its black forests and icy mountains, is where the first witches came from.

FACT FILE:

GRANDMAMMA

Occupation: Retired witchophile.*
Age: 86 – tremendously old.
Place of birth: Norway.
Width: Wide. (Not even a mouse could squeeze in to sit beside Grandmamma in her armchair.)
Wears: Grey lace (and lots of it).
Bad habits: Smoking cigars and ignoring doctors (most of the time).
Distinguishing feature: Missing thumb.
Notable accessories: Walking stick and a cigar.

*witchophile: (noun) a person who studies witches and knows a lot about them. Like Grandmamma, for instance. When she was younger, she travelled all over the globe trying to track down The Grand High Witch. Unfortunately, she never even came close to succeeding.

56

RATE A
GRANDMAMMA

You don't have to rate your grandmother,
of course. Just pick the nearest one.
Even an ancient auntie will do.

Once you've found one, use the following guide to award her Grandmamma Points. At the end, add up all her Grandmamma Points to see how much she's like Grandmamma in *The Witches*.

Age: Award 1 Grandmamma Point for each year.

Place of birth: Award 100 Grandmamma Points for Norway and 0 Grandmamma Points for anywhere else.

Thumbs: Deduct 25 Grandmamma Points if she has both thumbs. Award 1,000 Grandmamma Points if she has JUST ONE.

Cigars: If she smokes cigars, award 100 Grandmamma Points and then instantly deduct them because smoking is a very bad habit.

Walking stick: Award 50 Grandmamma Points per walking stick.

Grey lace: If she wears only a smidge of grey lace, award 200 Grandmamma Points. If she's covered in it, add 1,000,000 Grandmamma Points to your total.

How did she score?

0–20 Grandmamma Points
Sorry. She's not even a TINY bit like Grandmamma in *The Witches*.

21–100 Grandmamma Points
That's more like it.

101–500 Grandmamma Points
Now we're talking.

501–1,001,235 Grandmamma Points
Oooh. She's REALLY like Grandmamma.

1,001,236+ Grandmamma Points
OK, we're almost sure that she's the REAL Grandmamma.

RIDDLE-ME-REE

I have a Norwegian grandmother who told me ALL about witches.

That's why I know how to recognize a witch.

I met two witches before I was eight years old.

The first time I met a witch I escaped unharmed.

The second time I didn't.

My best friend is called Timmy.

I own two white mice named William and Mary.

Who am I?

Answer: I am the boy from *The Witches*. I'd love to tell you what I'm called, but I can't. You see, Roald Dahl never gave me a name.

It's true. You can search through *The Witches* all you like, but you will NEVER find out what the main character is called. Isn't that clever?!

TA-DAAAAA!

Witches turn children into mice. Everyone knows that. (Well, anyone clever enough to read this incredibly informative book from cover to cover knows it.) But did you know that a mouse isn't the **only** thing you're in danger of becoming?

It's said that a witch can easily turn a child into **ANY** of these creatures...

A SLUG

A FLEA

A PHEASANT

So the next time you see a slug or a flea* be very careful. You don't want to accidentally squish it under your shoe or squirt it with bug spray. What if it's actually Andrew from your class at school?!

---

*Pheasants are less of a worry. You're unlikely to stand on one of those by accident.

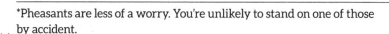

If you were a witch, what would YOU turn other children into? Draw or write your brilliant ideas here!

63

INSIDE

GRANDMAMMA'S
CASE FILES

During her career as a witchophile, Grandmamma discovered that witches do more than turn children into mice or slugs or fleas or pheasants.

They have many tricks up their sleeves. (Or possibly inside their gloves.) Read these tragic tales carefully and maybe the same won't happen to YOU.

The prize hen

Name: Birgit Svenson
What happened:
One day she started growing feathers all over her body. Within a month, she had turned into a large white chicken. Her parents kept her for years in a pen in the garden.
What happened next: She didn't vanish, but she did lay enormous brown eggs for many years.

The girl in the painting

Name: Solveg Christiansen

What happened: In Solveg's home, an oil-painting hung on the wall. There were no people in the painting, just a flock of ducks on a grassy farmyard and a farmhouse in the background.

One day, Solveg came home from school eating an apple that she said a nice lady had given her in the street. The next morning she wasn't in her bed. Her parents searched everywhere until at last they found her . . . *in the painting.* Yes, really.

What happened next: Every day, Solveg could be seen in a different part of the painting. Then, all at once, fifty-four years after it all happened, she disappeared. Gulp.

GRANDMAMMA'S
CASE FILES
continued

Yes, there are MORE cases. Stand by to be astounded and amazed (and maybe a little bit horrified, too) by the sheer nastiness of witches.

The stone boy

Name: Harald*

What happened: One morning Harald's skin went all greyish-yellow. Then it became hard and crackly, like the shell of a nut. By evening, the boy had turned to stone. (Granite, actually. For those who are interested, granite is an incredibly hard rock used to make statues and memorials. It's excellent for floors, too. It's less good if you're a boy.)

What happened next: Harald's family still keep him in the house. He stands in the hall, a little stone statue. Visitors can lean their umbrellas up against him.

* Did you know that Roald Dahl's father was called Harald? You do now.

The porpoise

Name: Leif

What happened: Leif was summer-holidaying with his family on a fjord in Norway. The whole family was picnicking and diving off rocks on a little island.** Young Leif dived into the water and his father, who was watching him, noticed that he stayed under for an unusually long time. When he came to the surface at last, he wasn't Leif any more. He was a porpoise.

What happened next: Leif the Porpoise stayed with his family all afternoon, giving his brothers and sisters rides on his back. Everyone had a wonderful time. Then he waved a flipper at them and swam away, never to be seen again.

**This is something that Roald Dahl and his family did every summer in Norway!

THE **SCARIEST**
WITCH-ZAPPING
OF **ALL**

Gosh. Where are the words?! Did they run out of ink? Should I take this book back to the bookshop at once and ask for a refund?

STOP. DON'T PANIC.

This isn't a printing mistake. It's up to YOU to invent the most jaw-droppingly terrifying witch-zapping case *ever*. Write the details below, and don't forget to be REALLY SCARY.

Who disappeared?

When did they vanish?

Where did it happen?

What are the gruesome details?

What happened next?

THE **CURIOUS** CASE OF
THE MISSING THUMB

If you've been paying attention, you'll know that Grandmamma has a missing thumb. The question is . . . WHAT HAPPENED TO IT?

Was it sliced off in a freak frisbee accident? Did a seagull snatch it?

Was Grandmamma giving a thumbs-up while having her photo taken atop Galdhøpiggen – Norway's highest mountain – when a sudden blizzard swept in and gave her instant frostbite, after which the thumb was sadly lost?

The truth is, *we don't know*. Only Grandmamma does. And she's not telling. So we've decided to let you make up your own mind.

Write your own brilliant story as to why Grandmamma has just one thumb. Make it as incredible or outlandish as you like. Add fireworks, leopards, tightropes, hand whisks and anything else you can think of.

After all, who's going to disagree with you?
Only Grandmamma.

WITCHES
ALL
AROUND

THE WORLD

'Wherever you find people, you find witches,' my grandmother said.

THE GRAND

Norway is the home of The Grand High Witch and all her Assistant Witches. (Important rulers are always surrounded by assistants, and witches are no exception.) But Norway isn't the only country where witches live. There are secret societies in EVERY country.

Once a year, the witches in each country get together in one place to listen to a lecture from The Grand High Witch Of All The World. This means a LOT of air miles for The Grand High Witch. Take a look at all the destinations she flies to every year. Will she be coming to a town near you?*

---

*If the answer is YES, we strongly advise you to go somewhere else during The Grand High Witch's visit.

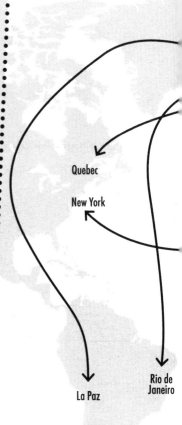

Quebec

New York

La Paz

Rio de Janeiro

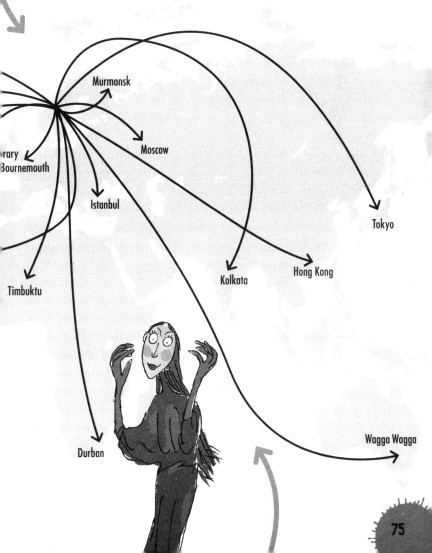

HIGH WITCH'S FLIGHT MAP

Murmansk

Moscow

rary
Bournemouth

Istanbul

Tokyo

Timbuktu

Kolkata

Hong Kong

Durban

Wagga Wagga

THE FUNNY THING ABOUT
NORWAY

'Where is the Castle, Grandmamma?' I cried impatiently. 'Which country? Tell me quick!'
'Guess,' she said.
'Norway!' I cried.
'Right first time!' she answered.

If you've read Roald Dahl's *The Witches*, then you will already know that a great many things happen in Norway. It's where Grandmamma lives, for example. And, of course, The Grand High Witch lives there, too. (Gulp.)

There is a reason for this.

Roald Dahl knew an awful lot about Norway. His own parents were Norwegian. Even though he was born in Wales, he spoke Norwegian fluently. And, just like the boy in *The Witches*, Roald Dahl travelled to Norway every summer. He and the boy even ate the same cheese! (*Gjetost*, a brown, rather sweet goat's cheese.)

In his book *Boy*, Roald Dahl wrote about his own childhood. And would you believe it . . . an extract begins on the page after next!

GOING TO NORWAY

From *Boy* by *Roald Dahl*

The summer holidays! Those magic words! The mere mention of them used to send shivers of joy rippling over my skin.

All my summer holidays, from when I was four years old to when I was seventeen (1920–1932), were totally idyllic. This, I am certain, was because we always went to the same idyllic place and that place was Norway . . .

The sea journey from Newcastle to Oslo took two days and a night, and if it was rough, as it often was, all of us got seasick except our dauntless mother. We used to lie in deck-chairs on the promenade deck, within easy reach of the rails, embalmed in rugs, our faces slate-grey and our stomachs churning, refusing the hot soup and ship's biscuits the kindly steward kept offering us . . .

We always stopped off for one night in Oslo so that we could have a grand annual family reunion with Bestemama and Bestepapa, our mother's parents, and with her two maiden sisters (our aunts) who lived in the same house.

Ever since I first saw her, Bestemama was terrifically ancient. She was a white-haired wrinkly-faced old bird who seemed always to be sitting in her rocking-chair,

Bestemama and Bestepapa (and Astri)

rocking away and smiling benignly at this vast influx of grandchildren who barged in from miles away to take over her house for a few hours every year.

Bestepapa was the quiet one. He was a small dignified scholar with a white goatee beard, and as far as I could gather, he was an astrologer, a meteorologist and a speaker of ancient Greek.

Like Bestemama, he sat most of the time quietly in a chair, saying very little and totally overwhelmed, I imagine, by the raucous rabble who were destroying his neat and polished home . . .

The next morning, everyone got up early and eager to continue the journey. There was another full day's travelling to be done before we reached our final destination, most of it by boat . . .

Fra Havna, Rössesund

Eneret A. Mathisen fotograf

me, Alfhild, Else Norway 1924

After breakfast, we collected our bathing things and the whole party, all ten of us, would pile into our boat.

Everyone has some sort of boat in Norway. Nobody sits around in front of the hotel. Nor does anyone sit on the beach because there aren't any beaches to sit on. In the early days, we had only a row-boat, but a very fine one it was. It carried all of us easily, with places for two rowers. My mother took one pair of oars and my fairly ancient half-brother took the other, and off we would go . . .

Every day, for several summers, that tiny secret sand-patch on that tiny secret island was our regular destination. We would stay there for three or four hours, messing about in the water and in the rockpools and getting extraordinarily sunburnt . . .

THE SECRET HEADQUARTERS
OF THE
GRAND HIGH WITCH

Somewhere in Norway, high up in the mountains above a small village, hides the secret headquarters of The Grand High Witch.

Unfortunately, unless you're a witch or a particularly talented witchophile, it is very difficult to find the exact location. (The clue's in the name, you see. It's **SECRET**.)

Use your navigational skills to find The Grand High Witch's secret headquarters, if you dare. **But be warned:** there are a LOT of wrong turns.

Answer on page 145

START

83

*RRR*ECIPE TIME:

GREEN-PEA SOUP

Witches LOVE green-pea soup.
And now you can make it, too!

Ask a grown-up to help you with this recipe!

You will need:

- A stockpot or large saucepan that will hold all the ingredients
- A blender or liquidizer to make your soup smooth
- 30g unsalted butter
- 12 spring onions, chopped
- 1 small potato, diced
- 1 clove of garlic, crushed
- 350g frozen peas
- 850ml chicken stock
- Salt and pepper

What to do:

1 Ask a grown-up to help you melt the butter in a large saucepan over a low heat.

2 Add the spring onions, potato and garlic.

3 Cover with a lid and cook over a low heat for 10 minutes.

4 Add the peas, stock and a pinch of salt and pepper. Bring to a boil and simmer slowly for about 15 minutes.

5 Remove from the heat and ask a grown-up to help you blend the soup so that it's super-smooth. (Or don't. It'll be just as delicious if it's lumpy.)

6 Pour into an enormous silver soup tureen and serve to a ballroom full of witches. (If you dare! Otherwise, serve in bowls.)

WITCHES' WEEKLY
The Grand High RICH Witch

Did The Grand High Witch inherit her fortune?

Is she secretly a bank robber?

Does she have a part-time job as an investment banker, earning oodles of cash?

It will come as no surprise that The Grand High Witch is MEGA rich. How else could she afford to travel around the world, lecturing at all those Annual Meetings? And secret headquarters don't pay for themselves. So where DOES she get her cash from?

In this sensational scoop, we reveal the amazing truth behind the world-famous witch's riches: **The Grand High Witch makes her own money**.

Rumour has it that there is a machine in her secret headquarters that is exactly like the machines governments use to print banknotes.

In an exclusive interview, top witchophile Grandmamma told us more: 'After all, banknotes are only bits of paper with special designs and pictures on them. Anyone can make them who has the right machine and the right paper.'

So, there you have it.

And if anyone can do it, why don't you?

Use these templates to design **your very own banknote** – fit for The Grand High Witch.

Front of banknote

Back of banknote

THE WITCHOPHILE'S
WITCHOPEDIA

Dogs' droppings
(Smellicus childrenicus)

Whenever you sniff a whiff of dogs' droppings, there are only two possible explanations.

1. You have trodden in **dogs' droppings** and these are now stuck to your shoe. Take a moment to make sure that you haven't walked the dogs' droppings into the house, through the living room and up the stairs.

2. There is a **child** nearby!

To a witch, children smell exactly like dogs' droppings. But here's the really crazy thing: *DIRT DISGUISES THE SMELL*. The dirtier a child is, the harder it is for a witch to smell them.

Here's the actual science behind this curious phenomenon.

Clean skin

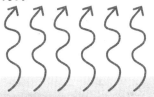

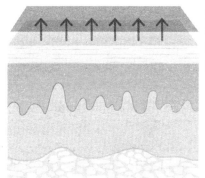

Dogs'-dropping smell of child floats freely through the air and goes straight up a witch's nose, causing her to howl with rage.

Dirty skin

Layer of dirt on child's skin stops the dogs'-dropping smell at its source.

WARNING: While a dirty child is less likely to be sniffed out by a witch, there is a danger that any grown-up who sees the child will immediately shout, 'GET IN THAT BATH. I'M GOING TO COUNT TO TEN...'

NEVER

ARGUE
WITH A WITCH

It is vitally important that you never, under ANY circumstances, argue with The Grand High Witch.

Ever.

Go to page 28 to find out what happens to anyone who DOES argue with a witch. It's best not to, though, as it's rather horrid. Just take our word for it.

How to avoid an argument with The Grand High Witch

1 Do **NOT** interrupt.

2 Do **NOT** fidget or wriggle about or pick your nose. (All these things will draw attention. It is much safer if The Grand High Witch doesn't notice you at all.)

3 Do **NOT** have any brilliant ideas. (That's The Grand High Witch's job.)

4 Do **NOT** be a child. (All witches detest children.)

5 If you are unfortunate enough to be a child, make sure that you are a stinky, smelly and extremely dirty one.

WITCHES' WEEKLY
WARNING
FOR WITCHES

Are you going to the Annual Meeting at the Hotel Magnificent? You are? Grrreat!

It's worth bearing in mind that Annual Meetings can sometimes be a **tiny** bit dangerous. We highly recommend that you keep up to date with the latest advice on how to stay safe while attending. The Grand High Witch herself has provided some helpful tips, published exclusively here. Isn't she a dear?

A stupid vitch who answers back

Must burn until her bones are black!

A foolish vitch vithout a brain

Must sizzle in the fiery flame!

An idiotic vitch like you

Must rrrroast upon the barbecue!

A vitch who dares to say I'm wrrrong

Vill not be vith us very long!

You may notice this poem contains no 'w' sounds. That's because The Grand High Witch doesn't say them. Don't ask her why not. If you do, there's a fairly high chance that YOU vill not be vith us very long!

95

DEVILISHLY
BAD JOKES

These jokes are worse than ever. (Sorry.)

What's the name of a witch's cooking pot?
It's called Ron.

Did you hear about the witch who turned green every time she flew?

She was broomsick.

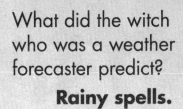

What did the witch who was a weather forecaster predict?

Rainy spells.

How do witches protect their skin on holiday?

They wear sunscream.

How do witches tell the time?
They wear witch watches.

97

RRROTTEN
RRREE-PULSIVE
LITTLE
CHILDREN

 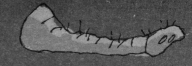

'Children are rrree-volting!' screamed The Grand High Witch. 'Vee vill vipe them all avay! Vee vill scrrrub them off the face of the earth! Vee vill flush them down the drain!'

HOW SMELLY ARE YOU?

It's well known that clean children smell like dogs' droppings to a witch. Answer this questionnaire to discover how easy (or how difficult) it is for a witch to smell YOU.

1. When did you last wash?

a) This morning
b) Yesterday
c) Last week
d) Sometime last decade

2. Do you ever use soap?

a) Always
b) Sometimes
c) On the third Thursday of every month
d) No

3. What's the messiest thing you've ever done?

a) Colouring
b) Eaten spaghetti bolognese without using a napkin
c) Taken part in a custard-pie-throwing competition
d) Bathed in baked beans

4. What do you do when a grown-up says, 'GO AND HAVE A SHOWER NOW!'?

a) Have a shower

b) Tell them you absolutely have to do homework instead because it's due tomorrow morning

c) Hide

d) Put on your trainers and attempt to break the land-speed record by running in the opposite direction

Count up how many times you answered . . .

a)   **b)**   **c)**   **d)**

If you answered mostly a)
Oh dear. A witch would sniff you out INSTANTLY.

If you answered mostly b)
Hmm. You're still in the **danger zone**. To avoid detection by a witch, it'd probably be best if you rolled in mud immediately.

If you answered mostly c)
You have achieved an **admirable** level of dirtiness, but there's still room for improvement. If you know someone who has a garden, offer to help with it right away.

If you answered mostly d)
Congratulations! You are almost totally unsniffable to a witch!

FACT FILE:

BRUNO JENKINS

Occupation: Child.

Height: Not that tall.

Likes: Food.

Favourite foods: Sponge cake, potato crisps, chocolate bars, bananas and . . . frankly, he's really NOT fussy.

Will do absolutely anything for: Six bars of chocolate. (To be honest, he'd probably do absolutely anything for a boiled sweet or a sausage.)

Nasty habit: Using a magnifying glass to roast ants on sunny days. (Gosh – what a mean boy!)

A CROSSWORD 100 PER CENT GUARANTEED TO MAKE A CROSS WITCH

Fill in the blanks to complete this crossword puzzle. Read the word in the shaded squares to find out what witches really, really don't like at all. (No, not even a little bit.)

1. The Grand High Witch hid her secret potion inside a very sqvishy _ _ _ _ _ _ _ bar.

2. Grandmamma's _ _ _ _ _ is missing.

3. To a witch, children smell of dogs' _ _ _ _ _ _ _.

4. Witches have _ _ _ _ spit.

5. Complete the witches' motto: *Squish them and squiggle them and make them _ _ _ _ _ _ _ _.*

6. The Grand High Witch's potion is named _ _ _ _ _ _ 86 Delayed Action Mouse-Maker.

7. Witches have _ _ _ _ _ feet.

8. The Grand High Witch turned _ _ _ _ _ Jenkins into a mouse.

104

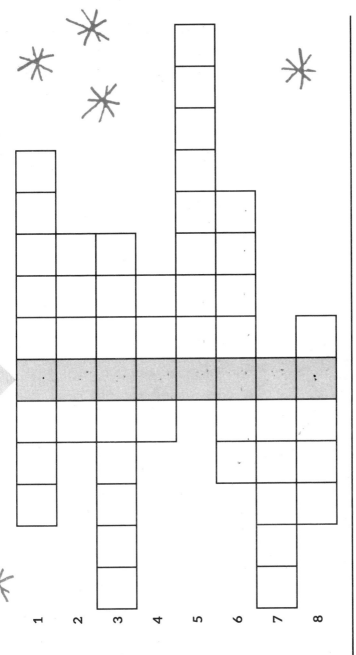

HOW TO
~~AVOID~~ ANNOY
A WITCH

*If you're particularly brave, don't just keep
out of a witch's way. Wind her up! (But
make sure she doesn't frizzle you like a fritter
or cook you like a carrot afterwards, OK?)*

**Things
to say**

I'll just go and ask my
WITCHOPHILE grandmother
if I'm allowed to eat this
squishy chocolate bar . . .

I had a bath ten
minutes ago. I am
soooooooooo clean.

Write your own!

Things to do

Turn up the heating. It will make the witch desperate to take off her gloves. And her hat. And her wig. And (if she's The Grand High Witch) possibly her face, too.

Take her shoe-shopping.

Suggest a manicure or a pedicure.

← Write your own!

. . . .

. . . .

. . . .

. . . .

. . . .

. . . .

. . . .

. . . .

MICE

'This smelly brrrat, this filthy scum
This horrid little louse
Vill very very soon become
A lovely little MOUSE!'

TWENTY BAZILLION* MICE

There are **A LOT OF MICE** in *The Witches*. That's what happens when someone invents Formula 86 Delayed Action Mouse-Maker. You're hardly going to get a book full of kangaroos.

Unfortunately, the mice have incredibly long tails and they've all become tangled together! Can you work out which mouse is the boy from *The Witches*? (*Psst!* His tail is the one with the lace-edged handkerchief on the end.)

Answer on page 146

---

*Approximately. The actual total might be nearer to 216, but that doesn't sound nearly as impressive.

THE GREAT MOUSE PLOT

Have you ever wondered what inspired Roald Dahl to write a book filled with scampering mice? You might find the answer here!

This is a real, true-life tale from when Roald Dahl was a boy. You might even spot a few similarities between this chapter from *Boy* and the story of *The Witches*!

One day, my four friends and I found a dead mouse lying underneath the floorboards at the back of the classroom. It was an exciting discovery. Thwaites took it out by its tail and waved it in front of our faces. 'What shall we do with it?' he cried.

'It stinks!' someone shouted. 'Throw it out of the window quick!'

'Hold on a tick,' I said. 'Don't throw it away.'

Thwaites hesitated. They all looked at me.

When writing about oneself, one must strive to be truthful. Truth is more important than modesty. I must tell you, therefore, that it was I and I alone who had the idea for the great and daring Mouse Plot. We all have our moments of brilliance and glory, and this was mine.

'Why don't we,' I said, 'slip it into one of Mrs Pratchett's jars of sweets? Then when she puts her dirty hand in to grab a handful, she'll grab a stinky dead mouse instead.'

The other four stared at me in wonder. Then, as the sheer genius of the plot began to sink in, they all started grinning. They slapped me on the back. They cheered me and danced around the classroom. 'We'll do it today!' they cried. 'We'll do it on the way home! You had the idea,' they said to me, 'so you can be the one to put the mouse in the jar.'

Thwaites handed me the mouse. I put it into my trouser pocket. Then the five of us left the school, crossed the village green and headed for the sweet-shop. We were tremendously jazzed up. We felt like a gang of desperadoes setting out to rob a train or blow up the sheriff's office. 'Make sure you put it into a jar which is used often,' somebody said.

'I'm putting it in Gobstoppers,' I said. 'The Gobstopper jar is never behind the counter.'

'I've got a penny,' Thwaites said, 'so I'll ask for one Sherbet Sucker and one Bootlace. And while she turns away to get them, you slip the mouse in quickly with the Gobstoppers.'

Thus everything was arranged. We were strutting a little as we entered the shop. We were the victors now and Mrs Pratchett was the victim. She stood behind the counter, and her small malignant pig-eyes watched us suspiciously as we came forward.

'One Sherbet Sucker, please,' Thwaites said to her, holding out his penny.

I kept to the rear of the group, and when I saw Mrs Pratchett turn her head away for a couple of seconds to fish a Sherbet Sucker out of the box, I lifted the heavy glass lid of the Gobstopper jar and dropped the mouse in. Then I replaced the lid as silently as possible. My heart was thumping like mad and my hands had gone all sweaty.

'And one Bootlace, please,' I heard Thwaites saying. When I turned round, I saw Mrs Pratchett holding out the Bootlace in her filthy fingers. 'I don't want all the lot of you troopin' in 'ere if only one of you is buyin',' she screamed at us. 'Now beat it! Go on, get out!'

As soon as we were outside, we broke into a run. 'Did you do it?' they shouted at me.

'Of course I did!' I said.

'Well done you!' they cried. 'What a super show!'

I felt like a hero. I was a hero. It was marvellous to be so popular.

A MOUSE'S-EYE VIEW

So, what's good about being a mouse? Quite a lot, actually. If there are witches around, it's honestly wayyyyy better than being a child. Here are seven reasons why being a mouse is just plain excellent.

1 A mouse can eat a fish-paste sandwich* before a witch even realizes she's accidentally dropped it!

2 Mice can creep into the larder at night to nibble all manner of treats.

3 Mice don't have to go to school.

4 Mice never have to visit the dentist.

5 Mice can scamper high and low.

6 Mice don't smell of dogs' droppings, which makes it far less likely that a witch will sniff them out (though it's not impossible).

---

* Er … yum.

There are seven mice hidden in this illustration. Can you spot them all?

7 Mice are awesome at gymnastics. And if you don't believe this, then turn over the page.

Answers on page 146

MOUSE GYMNASTICS

Yes, there is such a thing! What's more, mice are exceedingly GOOD at gymnastics. How else do you think they get into hard-to-reach places like the attic?

If YOU have been turned into a mouse by a witch, why not give these bendy-stretchy-twisty-turny moves a go?

The Triple Tail Loop

You will need:

- 1 extremely long tail
- 1 door handle

Wheeeeeeeeeee!

What to do:

Hurl your tail towards the door handle. Make sure it loops round three times so that you're secured firmly in place. (Your tail acts like an anchor, you see.) You can now hang there for hours, safe in the knowledge that there is no way you will come unstuck. **Well done!**

The Trapeze Swoop

You will need:

- 1 extremely long tail
- 2 door handles

What to do:

Once you have mastered the Triple Tail Loop, get ready for some serious fun. Perform the Triple Tail Loop, then start to swing slowly ... back and forth ... higher and higher ... higher still ... no, even higher than that ... **REALLY** high ... then let go of the door handle and —

flyyyyyyyyyyyyyyyyyy

towards another handle. Or a hook.
Something to hang on to, anyway.
Loop your tail around it and bow, mid-air,
to thunderous applause.

The Trouser Climb

You will need:

- 1 extremely tickly tail
- 1 trousered human

What to do:

This move is a real crowd-pleaser. First, run up one of the human's legs. Second, run down the other leg. That's it. The trousered human will dance. Your audience will guffaw. It's guaranteed FUN.

FLIPPING BRILLIANT!

What does it REALLY look like when a boy turns into a mouse? You could learn by studying illustrations of the different stages of transformation one by one . . . but wouldn't it be awesome if you could WATCH it happen? A bit like a movie.

Well, now you CAN – by making your own flipbook!

You will need:
- 7 rectangles of paper, 7cm x 10cm
- A pencil or pen
- A stapler

What to do:

1. Trace each of the illustrations below, numbered 1 to 7, on to the right-hand side of each rectangle of paper. Try to trace the illustrations so that they're in the same position on each piece of paper.

2. Keeping the pieces of paper in order from 1 to 7, staple them together at the left-hand edge.

3. Now flip the pages to turn the boy into a mouse!

SHOCKINGLY
BAD JOKES

These jokes are the worst yet.
We're awfully sorry about that.

Where did the witch
balance her teacup?
On the sorcerer.

Best
FROG JUI

What do witches
do at school?
Spelling tests.

What sound does a witch's cereal make?

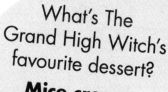

Snap, cackle and pop.

How does a witch order food to her hotel room?

She uses broom service.

What's The Grand High Witch's favourite dessert?

Mice cream.

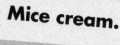

WITCH SPOTTING

As far as children are concerned, a REAL WITCH is easily the most dangerous of all the living creatures on earth. What makes her doubly dangerous is the fact that she doesn't look dangerous.

A QUICK REFRESHER

If your answer is ten minutes or more, we strongly suggest that you take a moment to remind yourself of the top five witch-spotting facts. Then check your immediate surroundings.

1 A witch is **always** a woman.

2 Witches **don't** look dangerous.

3 They wear first-class **wigs**.

4 And **gloves**.

5 And neat pointy **shoes**.

LOOK EVERYWHERE AROUND YOU. Can you see anyone who fits this description?

If so, **RUN AWAY VERY QUICKLY** right now and don't stop, unless your shoelaces are undone, in which case do them up immediately, THEN RUN.

If no one matches this description, carry on reading to make sure you really know how to spot a witch – *before she spots you.*

WITCHES **DON'T** WEAR
FLIP-FLOPS

Sometimes it's easiest to spot a witch by noticing what she's NOT doing. And one thing a witch will NEVER do is wear flip-flops.

Because she CAN'T.

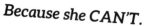

Think about it. Witches don't have toes. And, more importantly, they don't have SPACES between their toes for that funny plastic bit that stops the flip-flop from flying off.

So, if you ever see a woman on a beach wearing her best shoes, take to your heels and run away as fast as you can because **SHE MIGHT BE A WITCH**.

You might also want to look out for women who:

- wear **gloves** in summer;

- smile at children through **gritted teeth**;

- squirt on a **LOT of perfume** before going into toy shops to cover the smell of dogs' droppings, for example;

- and wear **exactly the same** hairdo every single day, without a single hair out of place.

Do you have any more suggestions to add to this list?

....

....

....

....

....

....

....

A WITCHER FRAME

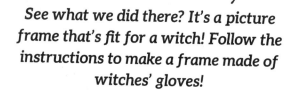

See what we did there? It's a picture frame that's fit for a witch! Follow the instructions to make a frame made of witches' gloves!

You will need:

- Card or a large paper plate
- Scissors
- Lots of thin card, coloured black or purple
- A pencil
- Glue
- Paint (optional)
- Ribbon or string, for hanging your frame

What to do:

1 Cut out a cardboard ring from a sheet of card or a large paper plate.

2

Draw round your hand on the thin card at least **sixteen** times so that the 'gloves' can be placed all the way round your cardboard ring.

3

Carefully cut out the gloves and glue them on to the card ring, allowing the wrists to overlap, as shown. If you want to, you can paint patterns on to the gloves!

4 Tie a piece of ribbon or string to the top of your frame.

5 Draw or paint a portrait of **The Grand High Witch**, then glue it to the back of your witcher frame.

6 Hang your witcher frame somewhere absolutely everyone will see it. **Especially** witches.

WITCHA-GRAMS!

Astonishingly tricky anagrams …
ABOUT WITCHES. Can you unscramble
the letters to reveal phrases that only a
witchophile would know?

1 DRAG WHICH THING

2 MURAL OF 86

3 SO EMU

4 SNOB REIN JUNK

5 MR AND MAGMA

6 ANY ROW

7 POD'S SPRING DOG

8 ICY WIGHT

---

1 GRAND HIGH WITCH; **2** FORMULA 86; **3** MOUSE; **4** BRUNO JENKINS;
5 GRANDMAMMA; **6** NORWAY; **7** DOGS' DROPPINGS; **8** ITCHY WIG

THE **PERFECT** DISGUISE

The best way to hide from a witch is to BE a witch.

We're not suggesting that you *become* a witch, of course. That would be a step too far. No, this disguise is much simpler than that.

Just **PRETEND** to be a witch by following these simple instructions.

1 Eat a cake with **blue icing**. (It must be blue. No other icing will do.) Afterwards, your teeth will have a beautiful blue tinge just like a real witch. It will be impossible to tell the difference!

2 Wear **gloves**. It really doesn't matter what kind. Woolly gloves should be fairly easy to find at the back of a drawer. Or why not look really fancy in a pair of long silky evening gloves? The important thing is to cover your fingers, so that witches assume you're hiding your claws.

3 **Scratch your head**. But not too much. You're pretending to be a witch, remember. You don't want everyone to think you have nits.

4 Wear a **hat** at all times. Pull it down tightly so it looks as if it's keeping your head on.

5 **NEVER** take your shoes off. Ever. Not at home. Not even inside Buckingham Palace. Unless the queen tells you at 120 decibels that you absolutely must take them off **RIGHT NOW**, of course. If that happens, obey immediately, but leave your socks on. That way you can pretend you have square-shaped feet.

6 **Sniff** every time you walk past a child. And pull a face as you do it. Make sure you look really disgusted, as if you've just smelled actual dogs' droppings. (**Ewwww.**)

THE **ULTIMATE WITCHOPHILE QUIZ**

How much do YOU know about witches? Answer the multiple-choice questions in this fiendishly difficult quiz to find out how much of a witchophile you are.

Remember: all the answers are contained somewhere in this book.

1 Do real witches . . .

   a) wear pointy hats and billowy black cloaks?
   b) accessorize with a black cat?
   c) ride on broomsticks?
   d) look very much like ordinary women?

2 What do witches hate?

   a) Brussels sprouts
   b) The ten o'clock news
   c) Children
   d) Semolina

3 Which of these items of clothing is a clue that the wearer is a witch?

a) A hat
b) A scarf
c) A spider brooch
d) A navy-blue poncho

4 What colour is a witch's spit?

a) Purple
b) Blue
c) Green
d) Magenta

5 What's the name of the hotel where the witches hold their Annual Meeting?

a) Hotel Smashing
b) Hotel Splendid
c) Hotel Superb
d) Hotel Magnificent

6 Fill in the blanks of the witches' motto: *Squish them and* _ _ _ _ _ _ _ _ *them and make them disappear.*

a) wiggle
b) waggle
c) squiggle
d) squash

Ahem. You're not finished, you know.
The quiz continues overleaf!

MORE QUIZ QUESTIONS!

7 How does The Grand High Witch hide her real face?

a) With an extremely powerful magic spell
b) With a large amount of stage make-up
c) With a black woolly balaclava
d) With a beautiful mask

8 Which of these insults does The Grand High Witch NOT use?

a) Whangdoodling nincompoop
b) Blithering bumpkin
c) Tomfiddling idea
d) Boshvolloping suggestion

9 What does The Grand High Witch do to people who annoy her?

a) Sizzle them like sausages
b) Pop them like popcorn
c) Toast them like marshmallows
d) Frizzle them like fritters

10 What number is the formula of Delayed Action Mouse-Maker that The Grand High Witch uses?

a) 66
b) 76
c) 86
d) 96

11 Who does The Grand High Witch first turn into a mouse at the Annual Meeting?

a) Mrs Jenkins
b) Mr Jenkins
c) Grandpa Jenkins
d) Bruno Jenkins

12 Grandmamma has lost something. What is it?

a) Her sense of humour
b) Her thumb
c) Her library card
d) The last tennis match she played

That's STILL not all. Keep going. You're nearly there! The quiz concludes overleaf!

YET **MORE**
QUIZ QUESTIONS

13 Grandmamma used to be …
- **a)** a witchophile.
- **b)** a Francophile.
- **c)** an audiophile.
- **d)** an A4 file.

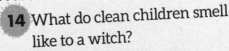

14 What do clean children smell like to a witch?
- **a)** Fresh blossom
- **b)** Cheese
- **c)** Sewers
- **d)** Dogs' droppings

15 Where is The Grand High Witch's secret headquarters?
- **a)** Wales
- **b)** Norway
- **c)** Finland
- **d)** England

16 Where EXACTLY is The Grand High Witch's secret headquarters hidden?

a) High up in the mountains above a small village

b) In a holiday bungalow

c) On the very top floor of a skyscraper

d) Next door to where you live

17 What does The Grand High Witch make at her secret headquarters?

a) Choc-chip biscuits

b) A terrible mess

c) Money

d) Beautiful tapestries

18 Should you ever argue with The Grand High Witch?

a) No

b) Absolutely not

c) Under no circumstances

d) Never

You've done it! HURRAY. Now turn over to find out how well you did.

141

ANSWERS

1. d
2. c
3. a
4. b
5. d
6. c
7. d
8. a
9. d
10. c

11. d
12. b
13. a
14. d
15. b
16. a
17. c
18. All answers are correct!

How much of a witchophile are YOU?

Add up your score to get your witchophile rating!

0–7

Witchophile rating: ABSOLUTE BEGINNER
Hmm. It's better than nothing. (Unless you scored zero, which actually IS nothing.) But we strongly advise you to try harder next time. You don't want to be turned into a mouse, do you?

8–15

Witchophile rating: SOMEWHAT BETTER THAN MEDIOCRE
Not bad. But definitely not brilliant. Put it this way: we wouldn't hide behind you if there were a witch nearby.

16–18

Witchophile rating: PROMISING
Bravo! You're definitely well on your way to becoming a fully fledged witchophile. Another forty-five years' study and you should nail it.

TOP-SECRET ANSWERS

Page 53: Formula 86
Word Search

Y	R	E	G	N	I	R	P	S	T	A	C	Z	D
G	M	W	E	Z	N	E	O	E	D	C	B	H	B
G	O	R	P	J	Q	U	A	O	U	G	C	R	Z
E	U	E	O	D	N	O	U	M	Q	T	O	G	P
S	S	H	C	O	J	Q	E	W	I	W	H	P	B
E	E	C	S	I	W	F	J	N	N	Z	S	T	K
L	T	N	E	F	B	J	S	M	X	A	L	J	W
T	A	U	L	T	G	R	I	L	K	K	J	B	E
N	I	R	E	G	E	C	O	A	V	N	X	F	B
U	L	C	T	B	E	A	S	R	R	O	W	A	L
R	S	B	B	K	C	O	L	C	M	R	A	L	A
G	U	A	D	O	L	G	J	P	C	Z	U	L	P
V	L	R	E	Q	Z	M	V	D	K	S	T	R	I
B	V	C	H	W	H	T	R	H	W	F	L	A	B
U	T	R	I	U	Q	S	E	L	B	B	O	R	G
Y	D	X	E	C	I	U	J	G	O	R	F	G	M

Page 83: The Secret Headquarters of The Grand High Witch

Page 111: Twenty Bazillion Mice

The bottom right mouse has the lace handkerchief.

Page 117: A Mouse's-Eye View

THE WITCH-SPOTTER'S
CERTIFICATE OF
EXCELLENCE

You've done it! You've learned all there is to know about witches and how to avoid them. And here's the certificate to prove it.

All you have to do now is *not get caught.*

Good luck!

----

was awarded
THE WITCH-SPOTTER'S
CERTIFICATE
OF EXCELLENCE

on _____

* *Did you know . . .?

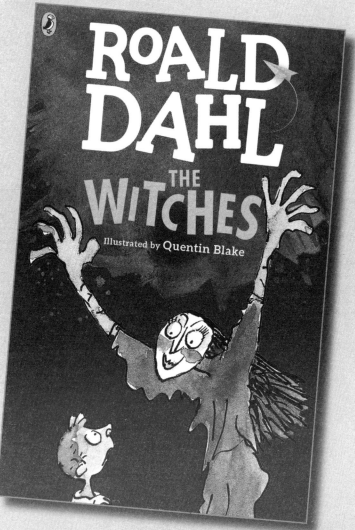

Roald Dahl's *The Witches* . . .

. . . is illustrated by **Quentin Blake**.

. . . was first published in **1983**.

. . . won the **Children's Book Award** at the 1983 Whitbread Awards (now the Costa Book Awards).

. . . has been broadcast on the radio, performed as an opera and has appeared on the big screen.

. . . will be a brand-new **movie** called *The Witches*, starring Anne Hathaway as The Grand High Witch.

. . . has **over 37,000** words in it.

Have YOU read it yet?

HOW MANY
HAVE YOU READ?

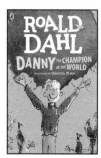

FEWER THAN 5?
WHOOPSY-SPLUNKERS!
You've got some reading to do!

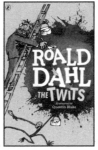

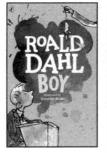

BETWEEN 5 AND 10?
Wonderful surprises await!
Keep reading . . .

MORE THAN 10?
Whoopee!
Which was your favourite?

ROALD DAHL DAY

CELEBRATE
THE **PHIZZ-WHIZZING**
WORLD of **ROALD DAHL**
EVERY YEAR on
13th SEPTEMBER!

JOIN THE PARTY AT
www.roalddahl.com